WHY TRUMP?

Republicans and the U.S election

Daniel Santiago

Daniel Santiago Publishers

ISBN-13: 9798343769609
ISBN-10: 1477123456

Cover design by: Art Painter
Library of Congress Control Number: 2018675309
Printed in the United States of America

CONTENTS

Introduction

The United States stands at a critical crossroads, faced with unprecedented challenges that are reshaping the nation's political, economic, and social fabric. The upcoming election is not just about choosing a leader but about deciding the future direction of the country —whether it will embrace progressive ideologies that favor more government control, or whether it will stay true to the principles of individual freedom, economic growth, and national sovereignty that have long defined the American experience.

The divide between conservative and progressive ideologies has never been wider. On one side, the progressive movement, largely embodied by the Democratic Party, is pushing for sweeping changes that promise to radically transform the country. These changes include aggressive climate policies, expansive social programs, and a rethinking of traditional cultural norms around family, education, and identity. Proponents of these policies argue that they are necessary to address systemic issues like income inequality, racial injustice, and environmental degradation.

On the other side is the conservative movement, championed by the Republican Party, which seeks to preserve the foundational principles of limited government, free-market capitalism, and individual responsibility. Conservatives argue that the solutions offered by progressives will undermine the nation's economic stability, erode personal freedoms, and lead to an overreliance on government. Instead, Republicans emphasize the need for policies that promote economic growth, ensure national security, protect constitutional rights, and reinforce traditional American values.

In this politically polarized climate, voters are presented with two starkly different visions for America's future. The stakes could not be higher, and the need for a thorough examination of these choices is more important than ever.

CHAPTER 1

Economic Prosperity Through Free Markets

The Conservative Economic Philosophy

At the heart of the Republican Party's approach to economic policy is a belief in the power of the free market. The GOP has long championed the idea that individuals and businesses thrive when government interference is minimized, and the economy is allowed to operate freely. Republicans advocate for lower taxes, fewer regulations, and a smaller, less intrusive government as the foundation for economic prosperity.

The conservative economic philosophy argues that when businesses and entrepreneurs are free to innovate and compete, it leads to job creation, higher wages, and better products for consumers. The government's role, in the Republican view, should be limited to creating a conducive environment for business growth by maintaining basic infrastructure, protecting property rights, and ensuring fair competition. Excessive regulation, high taxes, and bloated government programs, they argue, stifle innovation and burden businesses, leading to slower economic growth and fewer opportunities for workers.

A Track Record of Growth

Republican administrations have consistently implemented policies aimed at fostering economic growth by reducing government intervention. One of the most significant recent examples is the **Tax Cuts and Jobs Act of 2017**, passed under President Donald Trump. This sweeping tax reform reduced the corporate tax rate from 35% to 21%, simplified the tax code, and provided tax cuts for individuals across income brackets. By lowering the cost of doing business, the GOP believed that corporations and small businesses alike would have more capital to reinvest, hire new workers, and increase wages.

Before the COVID-19 pandemic struck, the U.S. economy was experiencing one of its strongest periods in recent history. Unemployment reached a 50-year low, wages grew for workers across all demographics, and the stock market soared to record highs. Small businesses reported higher confidence levels, and consumer spending increased. Many economists credited the tax cuts and the aggressive deregulation efforts of the Trump administration as key drivers of this economic boom.

Another important element of GOP-led economic growth has been **deregulation**. The Trump administration made it a priority to eliminate what it considered to be burdensome regulations, especially those that were seen as hampering business activity in sectors like energy, manufacturing, and finance. The administration's policy of removing two regulations for every new one introduced was aimed at reducing red tape for businesses and lowering the cost of compliance with government rules.

Lower Taxes, More Jobs

Republicans have long argued that lowering taxes is essential for creating jobs and stimulating investment. The party's philosophy is rooted in **supply-side economics**, sometimes referred to as "trickle-down economics." The idea is simple: if businesses and individuals are taxed less, they will have more money to spend, invest, and save, which in turn will lead to economic growth. When businesses have more capital, they can expand their operations, invest in new technologies, and hire more workers.

For individuals, lower taxes mean they can keep more of their income, leading to increased consumer spending, which drives demand for goods and services. This increase in demand encourages businesses to grow, further boosting job creation and economic expansion. GOP supporters point to historical examples of tax cuts under Republican administrations, such as **President**

Ronald Reagan's Economic Recovery Tax Act of 1981, which reduced the top marginal tax rate from 70% to 50%, and the **George W. Bush tax cuts of 2001 and 2003**, which also aimed at stimulating the economy by reducing income tax rates.

The **Tax Cuts and Jobs Act of 2017** under Trump is a more recent example, where significant reductions in both corporate and individual tax rates led to increased business investment and wage growth for workers. While critics argue that such tax cuts primarily benefit the wealthy and increase income inequality, Republicans contend that these policies lead to broad-based economic growth that ultimately benefits all Americans, particularly through job creation and rising wages.

Fiscal Responsibility

Another core tenet of the GOP's economic philosophy is **fiscal responsibility**. Republicans have long argued that excessive government spending and debt are unsustainable and pose a significant threat to the country's long-term economic health. The party advocates for reducing government expenditures, cutting unnecessary programs, and working toward a balanced budget.

Republicans believe that massive government spending crowds out private investment and leads to inefficiencies. Programs that promote government dependency, they argue, should be reformed or reduced to encourage self-reliance and personal responsibility. By limiting government spending and keeping the national debt in check, Republicans aim to create a more sustainable fiscal environment that allows for continued economic growth and stability.

In contrast to the progressive approach, which often calls for expansive social programs funded by higher taxes, Republicans promote policies that encourage economic independence and personal responsibility. By reducing the size of government and encouraging private sector solutions to social and economic problems, the GOP believes that it can foster a more dynamic and resilient economy.

One key aspect of this approach is the GOP's opposition to large, unfunded entitlement programs that they see as major contributors to the national debt. Republicans frequently call for reforming programs like Social Security, Medicare, and Medicaid to ensure their long-term sustainability. They argue that these programs must be made more efficient, targeted, and cost-effective to prevent them from bankrupting future generations.

In summary, the Republican Party's economic platform is built on the principles of free-market capitalism, lower taxes, deregulation, and fiscal responsibility. By allowing businesses and individuals to keep more of their money and reducing the size and scope of government, Republicans believe they can create the conditions for sustained economic growth, job creation, and prosperity for all Americans. While critics of the GOP's policies argue that they primarily benefit the wealthy and increase income inequality, Republicans contend that their approach is the most effective way to foster broad-based economic growth and ensure the nation's long-term fiscal health.

CHAPTER 2

Law, Order, and Public Safety

The Importance of Law and Order

At the foundation of any civil society lies the principle of law and order. A safe and secure environment is essential not only for the well-being of individuals but also for the stability and prosperity of the economy. When citizens feel secure, they are more likely to engage in economic activities, invest in businesses, and contribute to their communities. Conversely, high crime rates and disorder can lead to economic decline, disinvestment, and a breakdown of social cohesion.

Republicans argue that the rule of law is paramount to maintaining social order. Laws provide a framework for behavior, ensuring that individuals are held accountable for their actions. This accountability is critical in fostering trust among citizens, businesses, and government institutions. When law enforcement agencies are effective and supported, they deter criminal activity, protect property, and ensure that justice is served, creating a safer environment for all.

The GOP maintains that strong law enforcement is vital in preventing crime and preserving public safety. A well-funded and well-trained police force is equipped to respond effectively to emergencies, investigate crimes, and build community relationships. This commitment to law and order not only protects individuals but also safeguards the economic infrastructure that supports communities across the nation.

Supporting Law Enforcement

The Republican Party has consistently championed the

importance of robust funding and support for law enforcement agencies. In the face of rising crime rates in many urban areas, GOP leaders emphasize the necessity of investing in police departments to ensure they have the resources needed to protect and serve their communities effectively.

Republicans argue that increased funding for law enforcement leads to better training, improved equipment, and enhanced community policing efforts. These investments help police departments address the unique challenges they face, including responding to violent crime, drug-related offenses, and domestic disturbances. For example, the GOP has advocated for federal grants and programs aimed at equipping police with body cameras, advanced technology, and resources to combat rising crime rates.

Moreover, the GOP's support extends to enhancing the tools available to law enforcement, such as expanding access to crime databases, intelligence-sharing platforms, and community outreach programs. By providing law enforcement with the necessary resources and training, Republicans believe that police can foster trust within communities, leading to more effective policing and lower crime rates.

Opposing Calls to Defund the Police

In recent years, a significant movement advocating for the defunding of police departments has emerged, primarily within progressive circles. The movement gained traction following high-profile incidents of police violence, leading to widespread protests and calls for systemic change in law enforcement practices. However, the Republican Party has firmly opposed these calls, arguing that defunding the police undermines public safety and exacerbates crime.

Republicans contend that dismantling or reducing police funding is a misguided approach that jeopardizes the safety of communities, especially those that are already vulnerable. They argue that reducing police presence in high-crime areas can lead to increased lawlessness, making neighborhoods less safe for residents and businesses alike. The GOP believes that instead of defunding the police, efforts should focus on reforming policing practices, improving training, and enhancing accountability while maintaining robust support for law enforcement.

The Republican stance on law enforcement emphasizes the need for a balanced approach: supporting police departments while also addressing the legitimate concerns about police conduct. GOP leaders have called for reforms that promote transparency and accountability in policing, including better training in de-escalation techniques, community engagement, and mental health crisis intervention.

Addressing Crime Epidemics

The GOP has proposed a range of strategies aimed at reducing crime, particularly violent crime, drug trafficking, and human trafficking. These strategies are grounded in the belief that a multi-faceted approach is essential for effectively combating crime and ensuring the safety of communities.

1. **Strengthening Law Enforcement Agencies**: As previously mentioned, the GOP advocates for increased funding for police departments to enhance their capacity to prevent and respond to crime. This includes hiring more officers, providing advanced training, and ensuring departments are equipped with the necessary tools to effectively combat crime.

2. **Tackling Violent Crime**: The Republican Party has pushed for policies that target violent crime through a "tough on crime" approach. This includes advocating for stricter sentencing laws for violent offenders, expanding support for community policing initiatives, and promoting collaboration between federal, state, and local law enforcement agencies. Republicans argue that strong penalties for violent crimes serve as a deterrent and send a clear message that such behavior will not be tolerated.

3. **Combating Drug Trafficking**: The GOP has long focused on the opioid epidemic and other substance abuse issues, emphasizing the need for stronger border security to prevent illegal drugs from entering the country. Republicans argue that effective border control is essential for stopping drug trafficking and reducing the availability of dangerous substances. Additionally, they advocate for increased funding for drug treatment and rehabilitation programs to address addiction as a public health issue.

4. **Addressing Human Trafficking**: Human trafficking remains a significant concern, and Republicans have championed efforts to combat this crime through legislation and funding for anti-trafficking initiatives. The GOP has supported measures that enhance law enforcement's ability to investigate trafficking cases, provide resources for victims, and increase awareness of the issue within communities. By promoting collaboration between law enforcement, social services, and non-profit organizations, Republicans believe that more can be done to prevent human trafficking and support survivors.

In conclusion, the Republican Party's commitment to law, order, and public safety is rooted in the belief that a safe and secure society is essential for the well-being of individuals and the economic stability of the nation. By supporting law enforcement, opposing calls to defund police, and implementing strategies to address crime, Republicans aim to create a safer environment for all Americans. In doing so, they believe they can foster a society where individuals can thrive, businesses can prosper, and communities can flourish.

CHAPTER 3

Strong National Defense and American Leadership

The Republican Commitment to a Strong Military

A cornerstone of the Republican Party's platform is the commitment to maintaining a strong and capable military. Republicans believe that a powerful military is not only essential for safeguarding national security but also for ensuring global stability. The GOP argues that the United States must be prepared to defend itself and its allies against a range of threats, including terrorism, rogue states, and emerging global powers.

The belief in a robust military stems from the idea that peace is best preserved through strength. By maintaining a well-funded and technologically advanced military, the United States can deter potential adversaries and project power globally. The GOP has consistently advocated for increasing defense budgets to ensure that military personnel are well-equipped, trained, and ready to respond to threats. This commitment includes investing in advanced weaponry, modernizing existing forces, and ensuring that the military is adequately staffed and supported.

Furthermore, the Republican Party emphasizes the importance of supporting veterans and active-duty service members. This includes ensuring that veterans receive the benefits they have earned and providing them with the resources needed to successfully transition back to civilian life. By honoring the sacrifices of those who serve, Republicans believe that the country can maintain a strong military tradition and attract the best talent to its armed forces.

Foreign Policy Successes

Republican-led administrations have a track record of achieving significant successes in foreign policy, particularly in the areas of international relations and peacekeeping. The GOP has traditionally advocated for a strong American presence on the global stage, and its leaders have often taken decisive actions to address threats to U.S. interests.

One notable example of Republican foreign policy success is the **Abraham Accords**, which were established during the Trump administration. These agreements normalized relations between Israel and several Arab nations, including the United Arab Emirates and Bahrain. The accords represent a significant breakthrough in Middle Eastern diplomacy and demonstrate the potential for cooperation between Israel and its Arab neighbors. The Republican leadership framed these agreements as a step toward greater regional stability and peace, showcasing their commitment to fostering alliances that benefit American interests. This same interest and peace creation which is not common in today's government which has made the Arab-Israeli war lingered till date and has led to thousand losses of lives and properties. Also, the republican party has shown that America stands with the protection of human right and will never step on it, it also shows that America deserves the title of the world power, reason is because of their diplomatic way of tackling national and international dispute and recognition of other nation's sovereignty.

Additionally, Republicans have taken a firm stance against authoritarian regimes, particularly in countries like China and North Korea. The GOP has called for a robust approach to countering China's growing influence in the Indo-Pacific region, emphasizing the need for a strong military presence and strategic partnerships with allies. The party's leaders have criticized China's trade practices, human rights abuses, and military expansionism, advocating for policies that protect American interests and promote fair competition.

In the case of North Korea, the Trump administration engaged in high-profile diplomacy with Kim Jong-un, aiming to denuclearize the Korean Peninsula. While the outcomes of these negotiations were mixed, the GOP's approach demonstrated a willingness to confront adversaries while exploring diplomatic avenues to reduce tensions. These qualities were lacking in this current government which is the reason behind the current Russo-Ukrainian war ongoing.

America First

Central to the Republican Party's foreign policy philosophy is the **America First** approach, which prioritizes U.S. national interests above all else. This doctrine emphasizes the importance of energy independence, fair trade deals, and a cautious approach to military engagements abroad. The GOP believes that the United States should focus on strengthening its economy and ensuring the well-being of its citizens before becoming involved in international conflicts.

One of the key components of the America First strategy is energy independence. Republicans argue that by harnessing domestic energy resources—such as oil, natural gas, and renewable energy—the United States can reduce its reliance on foreign oil and enhance its national security. The GOP has supported policies that promote fossil fuel production and investment in alternative energy sources, believing that energy independence will not only create jobs but also bolster America's geopolitical standing.

Trade policy is another significant aspect of the America First approach. Republicans advocate for renegotiating trade agreements to ensure that they are fair and beneficial to American workers. The GOP's efforts to address trade imbalances, particularly with countries like China, reflect a commitment to protecting U.S. manufacturing jobs and ensuring that American businesses can compete on a level playing field. The renegotiation of the **North American Free Trade Agreement (NAFTA)** into the **United States-Mexico-Canada Agreement (USMCA)** is a prime example of the GOP's dedication to fair trade practices.

Additionally, the America First philosophy emphasizes a cautious approach to foreign military interventions. Republicans argue that the United States should avoid unnecessary wars and prioritize diplomatic solutions whenever possible. The party's leadership has called for a reassessment of U.S. military commitments abroad, advocating for a focus on protecting American interests while avoiding overextending military resources.

Cybersecurity and Emerging Threats

In today's rapidly evolving global landscape, cybersecurity and emerging threats have become critical components of national defense. The Republican Party recognizes that modern warfare extends beyond traditional military engagements and encompasses challenges like cyber warfare, artificial intelligence (AI), and asymmetric threats.

The GOP has prioritized the modernization of the military to address these emerging challenges. This includes investing in advanced technologies that enhance the United States' defensive capabilities against cyberattacks. The party advocates for increased funding for cybersecurity initiatives, as well as collaboration between government agencies, private sector companies, and international partners to safeguard critical infrastructure and sensitive information.

Furthermore, Republicans have emphasized the importance of developing policies that address the implications of AI in national defense. The party recognizes that AI technology has the potential to revolutionize warfare, from autonomous systems to advanced data analysis. The GOP has supported initiatives aimed at ensuring that the United States remains at the forefront of technological advancements in defense while also addressing the ethical implications of AI in military applications.

In addition to cyber threats, the Republican Party has focused on countering asymmetric threats posed by non-state actors and terrorist organizations. The GOP has advocated for maintaining a robust counterterrorism strategy that includes intelligence gathering, international cooperation, and targeted military actions when necessary. By addressing these threats head-on, Republicans believe that the United States can protect its citizens and maintain stability both domestically and abroad.

In summary, the Republican Party's commitment to a strong national defense and American leadership is rooted in the belief that security and stability are paramount to the nation's success. By maintaining a powerful military, achieving foreign policy successes, prioritizing national interests through the America First approach, and addressing emerging threats, the GOP aims to ensure that the United States remains a global leader and a protector of freedom and democracy. In an increasingly complex world, these principles will guide the party's efforts to secure a safer future for all Americans.

CHAPTER 4

Protecting Individual Freedoms and Constitutional Rights

Defending the Second Amendment

The Republican Party has long positioned itself as the staunch defender of the Second Amendment, which guarantees the right to bear arms. For Republicans, this amendment is not just a legal provision; it is a fundamental aspect of American freedom and individual rights. The GOP argues that the ability to own firearms is essential for personal protection, self-defense, and the preservation of liberty against potential tyranny.

Republicans contend that responsible gun ownership is a key component of personal freedom. The party emphasizes that the vast majority of gun owners are law-abiding citizens who use firearms for legitimate purposes, such as hunting, sport shooting, and self-defense. In contrast, they argue that calls for stricter gun control measures often unfairly penalize responsible gun owners while failing to address the root causes of gun violence.

The GOP actively opposes legislative efforts that they view as infringing upon the Second Amendment. This includes resisting proposals for universal background checks, assault weapon bans, and magazine capacity limits. Instead, Republicans advocate for policies that promote gun safety education, improve mental health resources, and address the illegal trafficking of firearms without imposing additional restrictions on responsible gun owners.

The party believes that protecting the Second Amendment is essential not only for individual rights but also for the security of communities. By fostering a culture of responsible gun ownership, Republicans argue that individuals are empowered to protect themselves and their loved ones, contributing to a safer society overall.

Championing Free Speech

The GOP has increasingly positioned itself as a champion of free speech, particularly in the context of what it perceives as rising censorship and the suppression of conservative viewpoints. Republicans argue that the rise of Big Tech companies and social media platforms has led to a culture of censorship that threatens free expression and open discourse.

The party contends that conservative voices are often marginalized or silenced on mainstream platforms, leading to a chilling effect on free speech. High-profile incidents of account suspensions, de-platforming, and content moderation have prompted Republican leaders to advocate for policies that hold tech companies accountable for their practices. This includes calls for increased transparency in content moderation decisions and protections for individuals expressing unpopular or dissenting opinions.

Republicans argue that free speech is a fundamental right protected by the First Amendment and that it is vital for a healthy democracy. The GOP seeks to protect the rights of individuals to express their opinions without fear of retribution or censorship. This commitment extends to the promotion of policies that encourage diverse viewpoints on college campuses and within public discourse, opposing what they see as a pervasive culture of "cancel culture" that punishes those who hold dissenting views.

By championing free speech, the Republican Party aims to ensure that all voices are heard and that the marketplace of ideas remains vibrant and diverse. The GOP believes that protecting free expression is essential for preserving the foundational principles of democracy and promoting accountability in government and society.

Religious Freedom and Conservative Values

At the core of the Republican Party's platform is a commitment to protecting religious freedom and upholding the traditional values that have shaped American culture. The GOP believes that religious liberty is a fundamental human right that allows individuals to practice their faith freely without government interference.

Republicans argue that protecting religious freedom is essential for maintaining the moral fabric of society. The party supports policies that safeguard the rights of individuals and organizations to express their religious beliefs openly and to act in accordance with their faith. This includes opposing government mandates that infringe upon religious practices, such as the requirement for religious organizations to provide contraceptive coverage in health insurance plans.

The GOP also emphasizes the importance of conservative values, such as family, personal responsibility, and respect for life. Republicans argue that these values are essential for fostering strong communities and promoting social cohesion. The party has consistently opposed efforts to redefine traditional values in ways that it perceives as undermining the foundational principles of American society.

In addition to defending religious liberty, the Republican Party has sought to promote faith-based initiatives that address social issues, such as poverty and education. By partnering with religious organizations, the GOP believes that it can leverage the expertise and compassion of faith communities to tackle pressing challenges and promote the common good.

Judicial Appointments

Judicial appointments have been a central focus of the Republican Party, particularly in recent years. The GOP views the appointment of judges, especially to the Supreme Court, as a critical means of safeguarding individual liberties and upholding the Constitution. Republican leaders argue that the judiciary plays a vital role in interpreting and protecting constitutional rights, and they are committed to appointing judges who adhere to a strict interpretation of the law.

The appointments of justices like **Neil Gorsuch**, **Brett Kavanaugh**, and **Amy Coney Barrett** to the Supreme Court during the Trump administration are viewed as pivotal moments for the Republican Party. These appointments have shifted the ideological balance of the Court toward a more conservative interpretation of the law. Republicans argue that this shift will have lasting implications for issues such as religious freedom, Second Amendment rights, and freedom of speech.

The GOP has also focused on appointing judges to lower federal courts who are committed to constitutional principles and who understand the importance of limiting judicial activism. The party believes that by appointing judges who respect the original intent of the Constitution, they can help ensure that individual liberties are protected from government overreach.

In summary, the Republican Party's commitment to protecting individual freedoms and constitutional rights is rooted in a belief in the importance of personal liberties, religious freedom, and the rule of law. By defending the Second Amendment, championing free speech, upholding traditional values, and prioritizing judicial appointments, the GOP aims to create an environment where individual rights are respected and preserved. In a time of increasing division and debate over these issues, the Republican Party seeks to reaffirm its dedication to safeguarding the freedoms that define American democracy.

CHAPTER 5

Immigration and Border Security

A Crisis at the Border

The issue of immigration and border security has emerged as a central concern for the Republican Party, particularly in the context of rising illegal immigration, human trafficking, and drug smuggling. Republicans argue that the current immigration policies are inadequate to address these challenges, necessitating a stricter approach to border security and enforcement.

The GOP emphasizes that a surge in illegal immigration can overwhelm resources, strain social services, and pose significant threats to public safety. Republicans assert that unchecked immigration leads to an increase in criminal activity, as human traffickers and drug cartels exploit vulnerabilities in the border security system. The party argues that effective immigration policies must prioritize the safety of American citizens and protect vulnerable populations from exploitation.

To combat these issues, the Republican Party advocates for robust border security measures, including increased funding for border enforcement and enhanced cooperation with local law enforcement agencies. The GOP contends that a secure border is essential for preventing illegal immigration and protecting national security, emphasizing the need for comprehensive strategies to address the underlying causes of migration, such as economic instability and violence in home countries.

Building the Wall

A signature component of the Republican Party's approach to

immigration is the commitment to building a wall along the southern border. Republicans argue that physical barriers are an effective means of controlling immigration and enhancing national security. The party believes that a completed border wall would serve as a deterrent to illegal crossings and help law enforcement manage and monitor border activity more effectively.

The GOP maintains that the wall is not just a symbolic gesture; it is a critical infrastructure project that addresses a tangible problem. Proponents argue that enhancing physical barriers, alongside technological advancements and increased personnel, will significantly reduce illegal crossings and improve overall border security.

In addition to building the wall, the Republican Party emphasizes the importance of investing in modern surveillance technology, such as drones and cameras, to monitor border activity and intercept illegal crossings. By combining physical barriers with advanced technology, Republicans believe they can create a comprehensive border security strategy that effectively addresses the complexities of immigration and enhances national security.

Legal Immigration Reform

While the GOP advocates for stricter enforcement of immigration laws, it also recognizes the need for legal immigration reform. Republicans argue that the current immigration system is outdated and in need of modernization to better reflect the needs of the U.S. economy and ensure that legal immigration serves the national interest.

One of the key components of Republican immigration reform is prioritizing skilled workers. The party believes that the U.S. should focus on attracting individuals who possess valuable skills and education that contribute to economic growth and innovation. By reforming the visa system to favor skilled labor, Republicans argue that the country can enhance its competitiveness and fill critical workforce gaps.

Additionally, Republicans emphasize the importance of securing the border as a prerequisite for any comprehensive immigration reform. They argue that before considering pathways to legal status for undocumented immigrants, the government must demonstrate a commitment to controlling illegal immigration and enforcing existing laws. This approach aims to prevent abuse of the immigration system and ensure that future immigration policies are sustainable and effective.

The GOP also seeks to address the challenges associated with asylum laws, advocating for reforms that prevent the exploitation of the asylum process by individuals who do not meet the legal criteria. Republicans argue that by streamlining the asylum application process and increasing scrutiny of claims, the U.S. can better protect legitimate asylum seekers while preventing abuse of the system.

The Impact on the Economy

The Republican Party argues that illegal immigration has significant economic implications that must be addressed through effective policies. Republicans contend that illegal immigration can strain social services, take jobs from American workers, and depress wages, particularly for lower-income citizens.

One of the primary concerns is the strain that illegal immigration places on public resources, such as education, healthcare, and welfare programs. Republicans argue that when undocumented immigrants access these services, it diverts resources away from American citizens and legal residents who may be in need. This situation, they assert, can lead to increased taxes and diminished quality of services for the broader population.

Moreover, the GOP contends that illegal immigration can contribute to job displacement and wage suppression. By allowing undocumented workers to compete for jobs without the same legal protections and obligations as American citizens, the party argues that wages can be driven down, particularly in low-skill labor markets. This dynamic can create challenges for American workers seeking employment and exacerbate economic inequalities.

To address these concerns, the Republican Party advocates for immigration policies that prioritize legal immigration pathways and ensure that American workers are protected. By promoting skilled immigration and enforcing existing immigration laws, Republicans believe they can create a more equitable labor market and strengthen the economy for all citizens.

In conclusion, the Republican Party's approach to immigration and border security is rooted in a commitment to protecting national security, addressing illegal immigration, and promoting economic stability. By advocating for a strong border security framework, building the wall, reforming legal immigration processes, and addressing the economic impacts of illegal immigration, the GOP aims to create a sustainable immigration system that benefits the nation as a whole. In an increasingly complex and interconnected world, the party believes that effective immigration policies are essential for safeguarding American interests and ensuring the prosperity of future generations.

CHAPTER 6

Energy Independence and Environmental Balance

The Path to Energy Independence

The Republican Party has long championed policies aimed at achieving energy independence for the United States. The GOP argues that the ability to produce and utilize domestic energy sources, including oil, natural gas, and coal, is essential for national security and economic stability. By tapping into its own vast energy resources, the U.S. can reduce its reliance on foreign energy imports and bolster its strategic position on the global stage.

The party points to the significant advancements made in energy production over the past decade, particularly during the Trump administration, when the U.S. became a net exporter of oil for the first time in decades. Republicans argue that this achievement was the result of policies promoting deregulation, streamlined permitting processes, and investment in fossil fuel infrastructure. By removing unnecessary regulatory hurdles, the GOP believes it has paved the way for increased domestic production, which in turn creates jobs and stimulates economic growth.

Republicans contend that energy independence is not just an economic imperative; it is also a matter of national security. The party argues that reducing dependence on foreign oil decreases vulnerability to geopolitical tensions and ensures that the U.S. can respond to global crises without the constraints of energy supply issues. In an unpredictable world, maintaining a strong domestic energy sector is seen as a critical safeguard for national interests.

Opposition to the Green New Deal

The GOP's commitment to energy independence includes a vocal opposition to the **Green New Deal** and similar progressive environmental initiatives. Republicans argue that such radical policies would impose excessive regulations on the energy sector, stifle economic growth, and lead to the loss of millions of jobs, particularly in traditional energy industries.

The party contends that the Green New Deal's ambitious goals, which include transitioning to 100% renewable energy within a short timeframe, are unrealistic and economically damaging. Republicans assert that the transition to cleaner energy sources should occur gradually and should not come at the expense of existing jobs or the economic well-being of American families.

Furthermore, the GOP argues that the Green New Deal represents an overreach of government authority, advocating for top-down mandates that could stifle innovation and entrepreneurship in the energy sector. Instead of embracing a one-size-fits-all approach, Republicans call for a more pragmatic strategy that allows for a diverse energy portfolio while prioritizing economic stability.

A Balanced Approach to Environmentalism

While the Republican Party emphasizes the importance of energy independence, it also recognizes the need for environmental stewardship. The GOP advocates for a balanced approach to environmentalism that promotes clean energy innovation without compromising economic growth or imposing burdensome regulations on businesses.

Republicans argue that the key to achieving this balance lies in encouraging private sector innovation and investment in clean energy technologies. The party believes that rather than relying solely on government mandates, fostering an environment where businesses can thrive will lead to more effective and sustainable solutions for environmental challenges. By incentivizing research and development in renewable energy and energy efficiency,

Republicans contend that the U.S. can transition toward cleaner energy sources while maintaining economic vitality.

Additionally, the GOP supports initiatives aimed at improving energy efficiency in existing infrastructure and promoting conservation efforts. Republicans believe that a comprehensive approach to energy policy can include a variety of energy sources, from fossil fuels to renewables, while addressing environmental concerns without sacrificing economic growth.

Reducing Foreign Dependency

Achieving energy independence is also about reducing America's reliance on foreign oil, which Republicans view as a strategic advantage. By developing and utilizing domestic energy resources, the U.S. can strengthen its geopolitical positioning and enhance its leverage in international relations.

The GOP argues that reducing foreign dependency on oil decreases vulnerability to global market fluctuations and political instability in oil-producing regions. By fostering a robust domestic energy sector, Republicans believe that the U.S. can exert greater influence on the global energy landscape, ensuring that it is less susceptible to supply disruptions and price volatility.

Moreover, energy independence is seen as a way to enhance national security by mitigating the influence of adversarial nations that rely on oil revenues. The GOP argues that by promoting domestic energy production, the U.S. can weaken the financial capabilities of regimes that pose a threat to American interests.

In conclusion, the Republican Party's focus on energy independence and environmental balance is rooted in the belief that a strong domestic energy sector is essential for national security and economic stability. By advocating for policies that promote oil, natural gas, and coal production, while opposing radical environmental initiatives like the Green New Deal, the GOP aims to create a balanced energy strategy that supports innovation, job creation, and responsible environmental stewardship. Through these efforts, the party seeks to position the U.S. as a global leader in energy production while safeguarding the economic interests of its citizens.

CHAPTER 7

Education, Family, and the Future of American Values

Empowering Parents Through School Choice

The Republican Party has long championed school choice as a fundamental principle in education reform. Republicans argue that empowering parents with the ability to choose their children's educational paths—whether through public schools, charter schools, or private institutions—enhances educational outcomes and fosters competition among schools.

School choice is seen as a mechanism to improve educational quality by allowing parents to select schools that align with their values and meet their children's specific needs. The GOP supports initiatives such as voucher programs that enable families to use public funding for private education, providing opportunities for children in underperforming schools to access better educational options.

Republicans believe that giving parents more control over their children's education promotes accountability within the school system. When schools are competing for students, they are incentivized to improve their services, leading to better educational standards overall. Additionally, the GOP argues that school choice can empower families in low-income communities, offering them access to quality education that might otherwise be out of reach.

By advocating for school choice, the Republican Party aims to create an education system that prioritizes parental involvement and fosters a sense of responsibility among families regarding their children's education.

Opposing Progressive Indoctrination

A central theme in the Republican Party's education platform is opposition to what they term "progressive indoctrination" in public schools. This includes the teaching of critical race theory (CRT) and other ideologies that Republicans argue promote division and conflict rather than unity and understanding.

The GOP contends that CRT, which examines the ways in which race and racism intersect with other social factors in the United States, fosters a negative view of American history and promotes a victimhood mentality among students. Republicans argue that these teachings can lead to a divisive environment that undermines social cohesion and patriotism.

In response, the Republican Party has pushed for legislation banning the teaching of CRT and similar ideologies in schools. They advocate for an education that emphasizes American history, achievements, and the principles of liberty and equality for all citizens. The GOP believes that by opposing progressive indoctrination, they can promote a more accurate and unifying understanding of American history that fosters pride and civic responsibility among students.

Supporting Traditional Family Values

The GOP has consistently defended traditional family values, arguing that a strong family structure is essential for a stable society. Republicans believe that policies should promote and protect the family unit, recognizing it as the cornerstone of community life.

The party advocates for policies that support marriage and family stability, such as tax incentives for married couples and programs aimed at strengthening families. Republicans argue that healthy family dynamics contribute to positive outcomes for children, including better educational performance and emotional well-being.

Additionally, the GOP emphasizes the importance of parental

rights in education and child-rearing. Republicans argue that parents should have the primary authority in determining what is best for their children, particularly concerning moral and ethical education. By protecting parental rights, the party seeks to ensure that families can pass on their values and beliefs without interference from external forces.

Fostering Patriotism in Education

The Republican Party believes that fostering patriotism and an appreciation for American values is critical for the future of the nation. The GOP argues that education should include a robust curriculum that teaches students about the country's founding principles, history, and the importance of civic engagement.

Republicans advocate for programs that promote pride in America's achievements and encourage students to engage with their communities and participate in democratic processes. The party contends that instilling a sense of patriotism in young people is essential for cultivating responsible citizens who understand their rights and responsibilities.

In promoting patriotism in education, the GOP seeks to counter narratives that portray America in a negative light. Republicans argue that a balanced understanding of American history, including both its triumphs and challenges, can help students appreciate the complexities of the nation's past while recognizing its potential for growth and improvement.

In conclusion, the Republican Party's focus on education, family, and the future of American values reflects its commitment to empowering parents, opposing divisive ideologies, supporting traditional family structures, and fostering patriotism. By advocating for school choice, opposing progressive indoctrination, promoting family values, and instilling a sense of pride in American history, the GOP aims to shape a future where families thrive, children receive a quality education, and the values that define the nation are preserved for generations to come. As America faces ongoing challenges and debates over its identity, the Republican Party believes that a strong foundation in education and family is vital for ensuring a prosperous and unified future.

CONCLUSION

Why the Republican Party is the Right Choice for America and Why Donald Trump Is the Man for The Job

A Vision for the Future

In conclusion, the Republican Party represents a commitment to a vision for America that prioritizes economic growth, national security, personal freedoms, and the preservation of American values. The party's core principles of limited government, free-market economics, and individual liberty are essential for navigating the complex challenges of the 21st century.

Republicans argue that economic policies rooted in free markets and fiscal responsibility foster innovation and create job opportunities for all Americans. The emphasis on energy independence not only secures national interests but also bolsters economic resilience. By advocating for law and order, the GOP aims to create safer communities that allow families and businesses to thrive.

Furthermore, the Republican Party's dedication to protecting individual freedoms—whether through defending the Second Amendment, championing free speech, or ensuring parental rights in education—reflects a commitment to the foundational principles upon which this nation was built. These freedoms are vital for maintaining a vibrant democracy and fostering an environment where citizens can express their beliefs and pursue their aspirations.

Finally, the Republican Party stands firm in its commitment to traditional American values, emphasizing the importance of family, patriotism, and a shared understanding of history. By instilling these values in future generations, Republicans believe they can cultivate a citizenry that appreciates the country's achievements and works collaboratively to address its challenges.

A Call to Action

As the upcoming elections approach, it is imperative for Americans to recognize the importance of their involvement in the political process. The Republican Party offers a platform that aligns with conservative principles and prioritizes the needs of the nation. To ensure that these values are upheld and advanced, citizens must take action.

Supporting Republican candidates who embody these principles is crucial. Whether through volunteering for campaigns, engaging in grassroots efforts, or contributing financially, every effort counts in promoting a vision for America that emphasizes economic opportunity, personal freedoms, and national security.

Additionally, advocating for conservative principles within local communities, schools, and workplaces is essential for fostering a political culture that values debate, respect, and civic responsibility. Engaging in discussions about the benefits of Republican policies, educating others about the importance of individual liberties, and promoting traditional family values can help create a more informed electorate.

As the nation faces ongoing challenges, the Republican Party presents a path forward that honors America's founding ideals and seeks to build a brighter future. By rallying behind Republican candidates and engaging in the political process, citizens can play a vital role in shaping the direction of the country and ensuring that the core tenets of liberty, prosperity, and justice endure for generations to come.

In closing, the Republican Party stands as a champion for economic growth, national security, personal freedoms, and the preservation of American values. By uniting behind these principles, Americans can navigate the complexities of today's world and lay the foundation for a prosperous and unified future.

Together, we can work to secure a victory that not only reflects our ideals but also paves the way for a thriving America.

ABOUT THE AUTHOR

Daniel Santiago

Daniel is a graduate of history and international studies and have always speaks the truth about the welfarism of his dear country. he is a single man who is not yet married because he alwayss dedicate his mind to writings about world politics, conflicts and resolution. this book is meant to shape the world and American politics forever.

www.ingramcontent.com/pod-product-compliance
Lightning Source LLC
Chambersburg PA
CBHW061546250726
48657CB00006B/2312